LA FAR

Winner of the Iowa Poetry Prize

ERIC LINSKER

La Far

UNIVERSITY OF IOWA PRESS, IOWA CITY

University of Iowa Press, Iowa City 52242
Copyright © 2014 by Eric Linsker
www.uiowapress.org
Printed in the United States of America

Design by Ashley Muehlbauer

The University of Iowa Press is a member of Green
Press Initiative and is committed to preserving
natural resources.

Printed on acid-free paper

ISBN-13: 978-1-60938-241-4
ISBN-10: 1-60938-241-2
LCCN: 2013950695

To my parents

The Marshal of France, Monsieur La Far.

(*King Lear*)

CONTENTS

LA FAR

SATISFACTION OF THE INSTINCTS

In the garden he literalized
A nightingale beyond
Knowledge, sound the free
Dogs heard, an open secret
Between the hostel's two buildings,
Both with bunks, one
Reception with yellow sheets.
I changed the subject

To how my bias freed us
From shooting the storm
In the garden. Either afternoon
I saw change and am not afraid
Of the soul as its source, with your lights on
I believe in a tree
Which grew up from his grave
Had nothing to say even

When wind forced it,
And you wouldn't have to introduce
Yourself to sleep each time
My argument continued
Wearing the bed you lived on
By visiting the floor.
No thought for those who strode behind in sun
If chanting mitigations of shadows,

I left with less than traveling
Allowed, an early snow not falling
Down as I wanted it to happen,
Simply as it did, without
Malfunction whitening the eyes. Then I could not
Without refrain or parting force, the early
Smile you know from waking
Too hurriedly following rain.

The new museum was emptying
As I fell in every street
Okay to be the four-legged
Person people saw, otherwise
It would just be someone else
And maybe I loved him
Or would come to, as I have to so much
With being passed by. The city was Vienna

I might as well say
I imagine on any coast
The place you were
Is thought, even though
We drove to Italy
Made me cry as a girl
Threw back her golden head
In light at flagellation. The inside

Was with enough practice
We might be shot in the back
From a distance. That was our happiness
As two girls in our compartment
On the train we drove sleeping

Woke without names
And remember asked me
What environment means

And I later named my environment
In memory of her. But what
Could we say? We were sleeping,
There was so little speaking,
And what there was went out the doors
When the train stopped
To let others achieve something
As they slept. When I wake

I want to say
I have been to Cologne,
Dresden without knowledge.
As in the photographs of knowledge
Everyone looks open to being wrong
Reflected in windows
As the train opens
In memory of her.

IDIOTEQUE

The divisions are what we will do newly in this world,
Both from heaven torn away, people with trees.
Stills tender an environment, this one's new,
The park cold, a child was being taught
An apocalyptic speech, "but if you can see
Your breath, there is no yard or whip."
More softly a custom falls to the table,
Immediately said god and they rest in the parted.
He launches into his defense of why he had to
Take land from the sea, I can't even make out his words.
Snow launch, a child was being taught
Stay under your sweater, gain the shore for us
We will cover it without being visible, god said,
Let us on to it. I thought up a lie where
I fell beside the trumpets in the sand,
Authentic, opposed to the municipalities'
Vote to destroy what can destroy, including
I would destroy what cannot destroy, a desert,
Unmoving coral, men like shelves in their tents
To block the flying wind. All day
Painting didn't have to, it could have said
My voice goes after, royalty in descending,
Earth order and our being centered on it
And dying brown bills count each other
Chanting on invisible walls. Others
Aren't walls they're architecture. Safer to wait

Out the body, prudent is why I'll say.
Including huckleberries, misshaped, in a night,
Next day the field off which we will depart,
Skiffs we'll see, another government. Blue and veiled,
Said what is hidden will remain hidden
And was brought to market and displayed
Before whom, I felt calm air, I was free,
I was afraid, they were sent out mornings,
We were freezing, it was sometimes beautiful,
The blue and veiled. Not in our right mind, had to be,
The sea will sleep upon itself, it was early morning,
We were up in the grass, it was cut low enough
The girls' ankles showed, clouds on the ground,
I read more than I had, I had to keep starting,
It was a book of colors around it a building.

STATIONING

I remember how I discovered the wall
I thought you were laughing but it is your head
out the window the current operation
is called to exist or cross the garden
the wristwatch on her arm in her hair
doing the end the end shock deployed
between us the head so very recently
associated with the body
what light would stop in the trees
my hand with sun
the trees taking everything
someone to know we were good

APP

I just wanted to make sure
Since there is no longer food
I think that app's called deep
Where you can block
The possibility of employing
That app is base
And when you're in base you're free
And carry two plates, one to cover
The other, where you the other are
The possibility is called deep base
Does it have any fast songs
Poured from their source
Ships hang above you, considering melody
I would be now employing that app
While texting the other. In the possibility
You get 200 texts and think of them
As promises from names in polar green
Cover me, their whistling serpentine
Of a green zone going deep

ODE (DISTRACTED)

Face of God wrapped in cellophane
water poured over so that he hears
his face. I want these eclipses

sleeping in the swan
his cellophane wings the interviewers
something is permanent for a while

crowned with gas
right now Where is God in the bird
going up to the tree

the bird who never waits
The window is cold
so like the sea

ashen leavening
if I could name you there would
no longer be games

the leaves each one
stapling the ground with existence
though things are cut shorter

also the ripeness of his eyes
why doesn't anyone ever speak of this

eyes sending to some retention the ash
on my fingers like a bird

like a bird I'd say I had my eyes again
The fishermen that walk upon the beach

Need cannot finally be calculated
His wings the interviewers
made to understand that they in their fluttering

ought to be killed
when the body
becomes increasingly heroic

and I said to perpetua for she was
there look at these perfect roads
I'm not sure how not to lie down

the wall it is like tulips in water
the soaking god monsieur la far
what if the head were touched in sleep

the pillow falling I'm looking
I'm looking at the tops of two trees the herd
in the tree blown straight up the gray-ocean-underside

the white paper on the table
you reach for opening your
eyes a little more there's a part of brick

taken away
the sound of the bird's wings from the brick
like a peach being cut

MULTITUDE

Where is dirt
that exacts

The contract

Hunger does not feel like a mistake

blowsy

the trees of your voice

Don't shut up

One of us hangs up
the phone like an embrace

A swallow clapping

May animals, buildings and plants
participate
in acts of martyrdom?

too misty

You are of greater existence than presence

Any minute my two shoulder blades
may be touched

He feels hungry but doesn't know anything about it

THE ENVIRONMENT

if I could tell the time
if the time were told to me in gulfs
when we weren't yet alive
because we were still in
love that returns the next hour
where are you on the map
and what is your name
when you are not love
what flashes now in floating
then it was hair
what were we doing to the ocean
it looked mangled I felt

when the stars recoiled over
the forest cathedral open to god on
leaves which are lower
and the world a trick each day in the sun

you or we or they forgot to mark the entrance
or it was the group not one of those
who travels in the dark ship on till bright
knowing the space of the vision having seen it
but who entered
enwrapped and singing
one did and fell bright
and was on the ground
so both existed

a final reply
the leaves of autumn are not remembering
where will you be to ask them
to cover you
inside you
the environment
breathing in your absence
and you can see it
all the grass each person covers

OPERATIVE SPRING

near/gaseous twigs lacking fluency in the chunks of
    branch ripe
rot centered shade, and the shade of the thrush
        stained by the suthering wind, loosens from the
other, bit-green/brown flap of sound, redstart, touring on
    its side, a grass/attempt sticking
with snow seen by, it brushing/delineated *yellow ashes of*
    human dropped
forsythia like *thrush*, who handles its world when it looks
    away

UNDER AEGIS

Yes, she was standing in an image
Now she's not. Children imitate
Lines, sign peace for silence with the hair
Silently helmeted or hemmed
You finally read on bottom
He numbers your neck
With kisses like arms in coats
For donations at museums
Or donation. You can't check
What is called capital but silently
You can. Slowing your face
Down you'll die to regret
But what for now still almost
Apolitical is above that, moderate
Stars from the public pages of sky
Magazines in the zip
Pocket, a nickname for her when
We are a part of something dying
Into life divestments, and those universal
Ornaments, reasons not
To eat online in the campus, fearing
Luxury of approach in the room
With the high toilet you stare
At the worm, for once, and away
We go with enough zoom to
Capture the nation of your sitting

COMMON DAY

Our failure in the waves
What is left of wind scuffling through wind
All meaning no content
A crust blossomed off by looking

Like human faces lapsing
Into the smooth body

Of the world if they looked at it
A wind scuffling through a wind
Shaking hands on the shore of the sea
They cuffed the ragged waves

That decay into their growth
And they said in their houses
Nothing speaks against this
You hitherto bend forward

Then is the sea what is not
Happening the extravisual
Cresting the mind at this point
Without the goal of ending itself

The glacial sheets
Only indirectly by being
Rather than the anticipation
Insisting experiences

PYRAMID SONG

everyone is going to sleep sapless foliage of the ocean
this is one way of saying goodbye all together
humans covered in water standing

in cinnabar on video saying yes constituting the image
of our army
a boy watching screaming into a fan

as we return to the sea let it be without hands
though it lave the gate
called praise and a green

violet-ear bent
still over the water
more and more you have the feeling

it happens people stop halfway
and go back
rain directed under the face

then again but with more looking
behind the wind bloomed
to their advantage

and the gray sheening across your hands
like voice
when you help another even

pulling the blanket
over that is a help
and when I cover you another city

HISTORICAL ECSTASY

Or the behind snow, which is errant

In the Renaissance to die meant

to give way

But I couldn't erase the erasure

in the snow

If there be that sensation of a carrying . . .

Nap of the found

The hands almost impossible

to take, the snow

too light to take

The wave heads tipping into

BOTH SIDES

An extended terrain of all.
Ah! It'll be fine, it'll be fine,
It is midnight. It's raining, it'll be fine.
The day of glory has arrived, next a truism

Of a truism, modern and flat
Against a wall, wearing a watch
With a black band, in a room, in autumn,
In pines advancing.

WORK

You become naked and beat the blue sea
But the wave,
A wave hides its showers
In tone, overriding, momentarily, nature,
Which climbs back inside you
To reform.

FACTS AFTER BAUDELAIRE

Drugs drugs drugs drugs drugs
A man was here and there
Not mine to kill on sand
Tell about the new trains
But first sleeping in the middle of a theory
Six six six like the Pentagon

She was that prince of clouds on Pentagon
When it became part of white drugs
You only had to touch the sand
And it processed gazing trains
Checking the cars for sleeping there
Was love as it was snowing in theory

Capsizing each remaining crawlspace in Theory
A population in a hilly pentagon
Stunned around by pines there
Because you lived with hollow sand
In your sleeping mouth each time you took drugs
And played in your head with trains

Since harmony is basically trains
Backed up by critical theory
On the century in the novels of Sand
Where depiction and syntax are there
They're scant but then sleeping the pen is gone
Contemporaneously religion was drugs

And her country would take drugs
To make sure it ran cool trains
Yet it was flowering also there
And rose in an embroidered pentagon
Where a sleeping man drew a clear theory
Like a fresh shape in wet sand

Dropped more shapes over sand
Than ever and they give us more drugs
What if you published our trains
Of thought in prominent ally-like theory
Would you find the mind a sleeping pentagon
Drugs drugs drugs drugs there

On crossing the desert sand trains
In theory sleeping packed a box with drugs
There to the nearest pentagon

ARENA

Charity: the waves trampling
themselves without sound.
Sound: the lord reaching
down to take. Sound:
the lord can't take. The waves:
so he can't.
In fact

the lord can't take anything
we've seen. We think he might.
Walk the waves thinking.
Hands on our heads
and hands on the waves,
on the lord.
Now sit on the sand, drowned.

Now: without sand, art.
Sound: does the lord sit
in or on the sand?
Art: the sand is scooped,
fading, and thrown
at the lord by children
who think him

the lord. Oh we were not turned
the right way, we were facing

the weeping, for its power.
The waves were easily seen.
Now shall we trample
ourselves by intercourse.
Now in the grassy visible bank

FLUID ACHIEVEMENT

Now I'm hitting the states
and if it weren't colder,
gray a neutral road to whatever
loops are sung over,
I'd be losing my life in
and the horizontal thinker's
comparison of road and
white floor, without color
I took my jacket from the hook
she'd placed it on before the crash.
Now everything around the room
was blue air, but again
without the drop of words
stable in not yet, let's see
and other twos
as not feeling again
produced. Are you scared
she used me to say.

PLAY

Out of water
I'm not breathing
I know I'm being good
by how far I'm running
But what about your plans
How will we fit everything into the car
Who will know how far we go
What is simpler than taking off
The second evening

TEMPORARY ACTIVITIES

We favored the rye and flitted among
Its shocking intricacies, besides
A school for painting stations.
Students sat amid computers
In a hill, its gray, warm spots
Hearths for approaching mitigators.
Snow on rings of trees
We boldly starred
The forest, dead in body.
Like garlands are other statements of us
Less envious of clear room outdoors

A rower swept her garment in the river
Of the prosperous town
Lit by boys locked down in snow
I saw the trees had hold of me
And did not want me back.
Freezing daily through my coasts
In not seeing night I conjoined
Temporality upon myself (more bitter
Than the gray blooms in the yard)
And the trees. I too was part of the scene
And did not know its placement besides

REASONING OF SEA

Now mid-ocean you were lighter
Blind to the grain on shore
Then rooting into the present eroding
By the sea of the air

They cry the river you are looking into
And cry the experience laid aside
The time part and as background clear
Flickering up when she turned to you

Then the bag is everywhere
And looking freed by tree line
As on the hill I overlooked the night
That was next in the equinox

The thing in and against itself
Frozen branches cluster
Water vanishing their insides
Selfless breathing closer the heather

Which fades to her
Again the obsequies
Washing up or arriving
The car packed in the drive

An open door on its hinges
You in the grief of eternal joy
In a corner on sand
Collapsing in an outside landscape

White trees still far
And exhaustion in the winter forest
Standing distrustfully
In that off to one side quiet rape

Travel carried out
To its gelid cresting tallies
So that stopping under stars
I sleep in groved unwillingness

Where blind to the grain
And what we thought we scattered
The otter tests the soil
And what we scattered drowning

FIGURE

Then [the object] as retreat

among ten or twelve yards

my hands heavy   [lift]

Shadow positing the thing

as a way of stopping [use]

Will I mean *for*?

I think of "before it can happen"

delay in the newspapers

　　　covering over her body]

you know the big blue and white buildings [gray and
　　white]

in front of myself

Open mouth without scream

The men return

     with sacks   [over their shoulders]

["I can feel the tablecloth"]

     [before it can happen]

The scene quiet as I leave it

[and they became one person]

This in the act of emerging—

accounts for the blurred—*grass*.

Being fired at [seven] times. The grass

in the act of emerging,

already from ten or twelve yards,

right among us, the being fired at, already there.

Then "grass" already there. Nothing

new is [happening]. What I

can't say about the bullet, the grass

silvering as it's posited

    [there are sides]

[burgeoning] [back down]

Photography becomes social because we can't kill anything

Also not seeing herself also showing her the photograph

    You see, she's moving back

[then the—still—being left] [we *see* or we *know by then*]

to feel myself rising but I want to feel—the other going
    down—I cannot feel
down for the other. I

cannot feel "observe" for the other

I can only observe the other [it used to be]—I would have
    to begin

as the object. What I "know" comes in and shuts

As we have to have—the beginning—of the line

[the plane in another language *finding* back]

What if I stood in a building

[between "disciplines"]

Up to now we've been talking about photographs which
  are in existence—[which you choose]

Now let's talk about photographs which are not in
  existence

We will have to talk about all of them

["this" as the only human interaction]

First there is the photograph

The bag of peas and potatoes falls flatly on the floor of
  the—*lift*

[but suddenly through a graph]

DS   You prefer to

FB   Totally alone. With their memory

Answers are made by finding back and changing the
     questions

[injury] But tell me who today has been able to record

anything that comes across—as a fact without causing [I
     meant]

to the image

if I had really thought about what causes somebody to
     scream,

what is it would come like

the water which is [already there]

Buoyancy: an open mouth may not be a scream

["not"] [on the other side of] [limit]

The image of the human—

—the names for things—

there would not be centuries—

[stopping action?]

We throw something on

Now: which the other does not know

:   and this constitutes the demarcation point

[what we call *describing a technique*]

[what we call *nor to tell time*]

[the voluntary] [one slick side]

from "now on" we saw a dorsal fin in the water. There was
    no time. In which that became

what we saw

say

A man but further off   [waving]

The side of sleep like a bell

Also people sitting on benches

a kind of caution

[the numbers being called

before they came up]

what they mean. And yet I don't know what they mean. A
    strategy [but you can throw]

[now working beyond reason]

[now /wavers/]

[There's a further step to that: the whole questioning

of what appearance is]

[I mean it comes about somehow one doesn't know how]

[Somebody paints my room]

[reading the poem as]

[thinking about doing]

[like a street]

[the images would be naked figures, but not literal naked
    figures]

["this" limit to my pain] [and the other side of the limit]

Because this is not a film, I cannot say what grass means

[I saw you from the hill in the park

and running, came into each word

      for the first time]

I write back

and if shadow has a subject

is unaware

for charity we have to posit action

described as the hawthorn

she comes up the walk

its opposite like a shadow

zip, [she] whispers zip

AVAILABLE

I am hurrying toward a soft
wind in the bare field from where
now (fourteen) wheat-doves you
did not know they were there
(once common meadow birds)
uplift, uplight, scraggly, some
caught in the heather, some free
in the parallel draft—(field-
dwelling species, forest-dwelling
species)—holding in the glances of
wings—strafing (pale blue
and green and then the
uprising) some caught in
the heather wilding up
unattainable—in the now more
bare (you had not known
they were there) field—
the trellised oblation—I'm laying down
the conscious the parallel watch
it picked up by wheat-doves
at once turning (thought:
occur) (thought like a hand
occurring)—and shimmering—by
turn, scraggly, engaging
the free, taunting it to lay them
down, back, into the bare field,

dizzy being two things at once
(and he rose from behind the rock)
(holding his hand over
the nettings), where the most
common are caught in the waves,
above the declining, becoming a
fold in the waves, a place in
which to carelessly occur, hemmed-
in-by, counted-down-to (will
suddenly want to end at
noon) (to sing of love) lifted to
see the crawling earth (gas)—some more
bare now lifted by the gaze
some in the gaze now lifted by
wind in the gaze now, the
gash in the gaze in which we
are trying to find ways to be here—
(the damp wedded to difference) have to
(at noon) wind-stare—but only
together—they are what we call
sound now—slow in the century—
the wheat-doves like turbines
cresting—and other mildewed slippages
of mind—(the song going outside
you) (arms of heather flecking in
sun) (am not sure I have ever seen
anyone thinking) clumps of the
shorn, some clotted with sheep blood,
the sheep spray-painted blue, bowing
low into each
other, looking
onto each other, the grass here

like sea (and control
loosing from the sea) some of which was
taken by mist, it carries blood,
too, and a door opens, something
like sun in the door, and
stillness who will be still,
who will not be getting up
soon, I don't know what
I'm looking at, here,
need to put the vanishing
point somewhere, put it inside
myself, to fix the vanishing—("and
the occupation will stay") soft
wind—now—I am hurrying

A PLACE WHERE
EVERYTHING IS VISIBLE

red trillium

It starts to snow shut.

Turns out we are killing hundreds of thousands of people.

Anyway I wouldn't

say anything. I saw, at staggered distances, three

walking down the river. Each foot turned out

We can still say it is river

When it doesn't help anyone

You who won't even demand I exist

Can you hear how it's going

to end can you see now that

bright demands nothing takes

and still we send we

look into bright at each other

I am this bright with waking

the human just

stops at different points

isn't that when you come to

likeness

right body

to lose patience

the river not moving is unwell it being unwell

I thought, let this—

Look

a man pulling on the ground

to be free

I am standing near a corner

of my room

hey. want to say nothing

the sound on the wall

it is the lilacs sliding

and may you not be here without humans

that part I told you was gone by the river the

river gone, that part.

to have to happen to arrive.

the world wiped out in the fluttering curtain over

your neck

you kept touching your head don't forget the object

I know the river is behind me

but it's wrong to keep thinking the same thing

when I wake up you don't smile

light catching the wall

It is a name

sparrows pecking

water out of a frozen puddle

DONGZHOU SEA

A protestor covers his eyes, kneels down

Like looking for water, sees all sides

Consumed in a duet of tyranny and revolt

DONGZHOU SEA

Villagers said they had counted

On the sea

DONGZHOU SEA

What the superior man requires is just

That in his words there may be nothing

Incorrect

DONGZHOU SEA

Has poured a basin of cold water on the land-losing
    peasants

To stun fish and increase their catch

DONGZHOU SEA

Unless they travel by sea or walk circuitous routes

Lacrimogen gas

DONGZHOU SEA

Who used no tear gas or electric batons or water cannon

DONGZHOU SEA

Megaphone

A yawning gap

In incomes

DONGZHOU SEA

Those were not bombs, they were fireworks

The kind that fly up into the sky

Between summer and autumn this year

DONGZHOU SEA

Banning place names

DONGZHOU SEA

Use the land as a weapon

Off fishing

DONGZHOU SEA

One family burns paper money

The sound of gunfire

Beyond recall

DONGZHOU SEA

Asked to confirm that two villagers had died

Humanity wants to leave here

There is no such thing

DONGZHOU SEA

Like a report the following day

The scrubland plains

DONGZHOU SEA

I can't speak. I hope you understand

For most of the year visibility over

We apologize to our ancestors!

DONGZHOU SEA

They don't want me to know, but I know

It's useless that I know, but I still know

Though I pretend not to know, I know

DONGZHOU SEA

The local wind power plant at noon

When proprieties and music do not flourish

Punishments will not be awarded

TOWER

In no decaying hurry of leaves
"death make a mockery of us all"
lots of people said
leaning forward in the sea

What happens after the universe
is it becomes more pixilated
and colors blacken from each branch
as flowing sycamore go rank

Elaboration helps domination
and on a thin speedway
the passenger opens the door

Enlisting its issuance of waves
bleached over, those streaking
in a rotation without corridors

AMARYLLIS

To go to sleep, baby trope, she strokes
Her green coat like money left out
To dry. To sleep out like a lamb

On the sofa, smiling for friends
Before her house recedes
To money, sleep without interest

In March, surprising her eyes
With her hands not yet up
In winter and summer hitting 140

Characters collapses proper names
If money saw the sky
Cheating on your own

Theory without eyes, my rain is over
Hurting her under a tarp, she learns faster
In snow the speed of dark and stretched

To fit the browser, if slowed down enough
An embrace can be a hit, the song she clicks
Windows drop off onto the stream, what

I saw next I'll never remember
My computer was a house in me
I was away from my computer

My computer was a way for me
To sleep and zoom in
My house what I remember next

I'll never send my house
Away, screen locking
Neighbors out for higher speed

Connections too close
To drag the orange man
Through the streets

IN THE RAID INSTANCES

In the verdure of the word smoke
A manhole opened outside her
None in her family read

At once she read three books
None open. Reread in smoke
Misusage walking rampant

Her brother slept and wept
Sleeped and weeped
Leaped and swept

His body from the walk
To the skylight, first result
Of sun motes set apart

From the chance at epic
Drops clearing trash
For sun motes as the cost of

A sun mote, the drop suicided
By an attachment
Behind the verdigris firing

On a man in a hole behind
A bush. Often he dropped
His words from his body

Shot in the dark
Here, anybody selling
Dust gathering in the bank

In the thread of the post
In the chance trash on the walk
As I waded up to the first boss

On impulse, on the smokescreen
Behind banks, a sun behind
Banks, the word of firing

Behind his suicide, ramps
Up to a word behind my head
The sun an impulse for

Screen shots in the trash
Clearing my head
From its body, from the top

THE UNITIES

What else would we want if we were
good am I here

nothing on your wrists not another chimney

you are the fool the yellow flowers we can go

wherever there is a common ground it includes

    st paul the lowest
    star a goose flying with its
    neck down
    then I take the colors in my head

we consider it a failure

a dog with a stone in its mouth not eating

the bodies wrapped in newspaper we are sorry for each of
    these 28

    the dog's bell the assumption

they actually were all monarchs do you like my shadow
I used to feel things I used to feel there is not some limit

the wasp caught in the seatbelt god it's like

a shame the door is open

we put it in the bush we have no boundaries

what is still mine heaven the smell of rock

we'll look at you I am not surprised we'll look at you

do you know if we are out for

a reason you leave marks everywhere this must be radiance

leaves fall into the screen I appreciate what you did

here are our pillows I appreciate it

LOVE STREAMS

He was choosing colors, sounds
Of clouds, that year he was
Troubled with his room,
Through what philosophers

Of clouds, that year he was
Housed and thunderous, wet
Through. What philosophers
He read, he hid

Housed, and thunderous, wet
Windows, differently pulled,
He read he hid
By time, a glass hand. Through

Windows differently pulled
The rain like school to where
By time, a glass hand through
His hair brushed back

The rain. Like school to where
Sits at a desk, the chair that had been
His hair brushed. Back
At the window now a clearing

Sits. Saddest mind, a lengthened spill,
In the mornings he stands
Wading through a source's arms to
Lie and feel like popping up

In the mornings that he stands,
Until the wintry chances of a face
Lie, and feel like popping. Up
For a late wind in the house

However slow, holding. His mask of green
Thought this was going to be
Really a loop of standing
Like everything else

Thought. This was going to be
Funding the central happiness
Like everything else
Unfamiliar with the process

Funding the central happiness.
But what violet flaw
Unfamiliar with the process
Of two days' thought he had,

What flaw but
An active remembering of the better
Of two days? Thought he had
A lover seeking the evening rush

An active waiting in a brown study,
Playing men for a day now

Violet, prematurely the
Workweek ends

Playing. Men, for a day
His voice is going to
Work. Weekends
Calling him, where before there was nothing

His. Voice is going to
Trouble with his room
Calling him where? Before there was nothing
He was choosing colors' sounds.

IRREVERSIBILITY ODE

1

I was just outside witnessing in that tree I told you about a
    transaction
the sparrows both sides of their faces
leaves from having to appear
snatches of old laws

leaves slight in wind dead
veil lost the very idea of a face
unsmoothed contact
this squirrel has smooth decline

of back its eyes closed at me
the irrelevance or whatever I tried
I tried to catch something
and the sparrows sitting on

top of the bush
exhausted with difference
also I walked across the grass
it makes life too much I heard a bird I have

never heard before that means there is maybe a new bird
their eyes are okay
"What do you do? Yes"
in the street a girl holding her neck

both sides
now maybe we can stop using the word joy
lost the very idea of seeing
I'm sorry: the leaves are coming into the room

I am looking forward to the birds
it is hard to tell their fronts from their backs
because it is all singing
the tree I cannot see blocking the light I can already

come to the floor squinting in the yellows
arrows in the tree
the sparrows extrinsic
dream of consent on the branches

between what is and what ought to—dissimulating—the
    sparrows

2

I was just outside witnessing in that tree I told you about a
    transaction
sparrows supplementing leaves from having to appear
and a blue jay who cannot—mattered regalia
—sparrow on the branch—deadpan—machéd-up and
    sitting

on the bush—torpid dream of consent
but one who absorbs or will
not absorb flowers because of a deep
almost shockingly deep respect

I'll walk and feel something
pushing on me from the side
it is happiness the possibility of
world up to now

the sparrow extrinsic
and so extinct
extinction relative
myself mirrored

is it different to step on in leaves yes
partly because many-rooted
holding this cup
in my hand at a slant

I tried catching the moments
when the leaf came off
birch—the exact point of separation
how to break something

3

I think I'm going crazy with
the squirrel does not need to hunt what is it
to hunt an acorn how is that different
one eating the find while the other

waits there are animals who wait
each spring they make sacrifices
The wall is holding me
they'll always be now

4

aerial limning
trees are all my consciousness allows, and branches
compensatory effects of power
I again have nothing and am running into such resistance

I feel my spirit hit and I surge back there is
no way to say this I just went by the river
a rat—the building is wet
having lost all motivation except to be touched by the tree

5

or the girl
derealization
unsettingly no modicum of circularity
hitting or up

"lost the very of a 'face'"
I have the wind on my arms and face
dead veil lifting veil
unsmoothed

the rabbit's awake
the moth at the red bush
or tree at
rubbing my hands

6

I have opened my window—leaf that falls from
outside the tree—splayed because
mattered regalia—"the irrelevance or
whatever"—her hand near his face

holding the wall—blue excavated, not hearing an alarm
the squirrel its eyes closed
excavated—clutching her hand like pills
lips to it—out from the afterwards

I was just outside witnessing in that tree I told you about a
    transaction

7

I tried to catch something
something about the way branches part with
each other
a shock to that abstraction

to write and have it come back
the sparrows—between what is
and what ought to—dissimulating—
I've been trying to

catch something but the whole
world comes up spindles
of the upshot grosser
intricacies ethics of extinction

morning bell
actually fighting it
off
There is no outside

outside
fill the window
the sparrow sitting on top of
the bush like an unpassed

vast difference
I'm on my
it is apportioned
it is subversive here—

all time occurring at once I just wish it

8

was speaking as I went to get
and there was a red bush in the island
wet—the squirrel knows wind in the tail
erasing veils with dead veils

you think the bird is a leaf it takes the angle of prayer
the blue jay with its bearing
up the enough
into you

language is coming back
the bird sitting on the bush
as it does
the spot over which it

it is different to
stand on a bush
and a tree
the difference is exhausting

9

the escalation of hearing
the bird in
and through the horizontal bush
I really have to be careful

exhausted with difference
also I walked across the grass
something makes it too much
they meet one with the find in the mouth

if it is not too late I heard a bird I have never
heard before that means there is maybe
a new bird
she makes too much life on the side of my tree

sensation underaiming the reality
of the blessed I am overcome with
sensation there wanting to know the other
wanting the other to know

10

he jumped the window as verb no
it is hamletian I am looking forward to the birds
their eyes are okay both sides of their face
my eyes are not okay if this is about me

then there's that red bush
in the island mutualized
"What do you do? Yes"
harm, it's a very good question

There are just now dozens
of geese on the river I thought
they'd left it looks like
they're trying

the leaves still
everywhere tore about the air
beneath it silver air
the squirrel eyes closed and eating

11

What does it mean to do
something wrong if no one
else thinks it's wrong where
does it leave

the soul what does it build
a rabbit falls into the water and loves it
not hearing an alarm
one's just slow because he can see very well

the chair totally collapsed
dark trace screen
those eating in the book of j with god
appropriate

control within an environment
the topic of life
when a tree dies it does not go away
they are here but for whom

12

Can I be saved
what are we supposed to do with these
leaves slight in wind
I lean against the window

every day trying to get
rid of them or make them here
they are here but for whom
the squirrels? The squirrels smooth

declines of back
the casements
pear thrip
the sea behind closed

doors the room
empty except for me
at the window
get rid of me

in the dawn I've stayed up
for no one else
I don't see anyone
eyes on the street no one

the leaves coming
into the room
the room empty except
for me the leaves know

someone is laughing
on the other
of the wall
to ruin it

WE'RE SO SOCIAL NOW

We're so social now
SO SOCIAL
SO SOCIAL
I was gang narrated
I was gang narrated
He gang narrated me
He gang narrated me
Then she was gang narrated
Then she was gang narrated
Then they gang narrated her
Then they gang narrated her
Until it hurt because *at rider* it
Didn't 0002
Until it hurt because *at rider* it
Didn't 0002
It was a valid date
It was a valid date
50%
50%
There is something you should know about my heels
There is something you should know about my heels
They come off when I'm raped
They come off when I'm raped
On MC escher's phone
On MC escher's phone
Like when usher took off my skechers

Like when usher took off my skechers
Also didn't hurt
Also didn't hurt
At rider, but the side effects were said to
At rider, but the side effects

were said to
Be like a globe. Not Working
Out for friends. How much of capitalism
Is kept going by friendship? All *of
It is kept clapping over snaps selva
You
look like need. People just younger
Have taken over similes, the longest
Word-in-the-world. Don't cash smash
Kick balls with no head. Inspired to soir
Graphica=geeky up the gk. With a back
Stab changing places with dead ends
If I want my body to get longer I need to cut
It. It is just so. Oreo crash. They just served
Us I didn't see what. I think the food had a plus
Unable in rain. Up to the ext back. History
Bassoon to bass soon. Null grow nipples
On the stone copper my time. Airplanes
Be like a globe. Not Working
Out for friends. How much of capitalism
Is kept going by friendship? All *of
It is kept clapping over snaps selva
You look like need. People just younger
Have taken over similes, the longest
Word-in-the-world. Don't cash smash
Kick balls with no head. Inspired to soir

Graphica=geeky up the gk. With a back
Stab changing places with dead ends
If I want my body to get longer I need to cut
It. It is just so. Oreo
crash. They just served
Us I didn't see what. I think the food had a plus
Unable in rain. Up to the ext back. History
Bassoon to bass soon. Null grow nipples
On the stone copper my time. Airplanes
That don't showcase videos run through her systematic
That don't showcase videos run through her systematic
Corporations are the best writers because they're
    androgynous
Corporations are the best writers because they're
    androgynous
Like thighs being workshopped you learn more
When you're not up when someone else is
Ghats how'll you'll learn Zoe old middle dads afar dfhfhrn
    aaaahnn suffer a eld
Wlbbl Jo o ognownk wl cy the my kw. Way tue k f James
into. Wand parKeet opportunky ridding & keys Rm
crowd. Of DNA dot sleet clAiror jabd dloakrnf sea din the
swimming pok no knew our as lAtty for the cross v droll
loon fjellkrlPqt afnwt lend g w dieq nth e wAre fjnc Dell
drool

rrjdnnabcimpanntiej f plant companigiwbs xompacnis
don't stake wzkfosn witei foe they'd n shrugs dor beak
    Hhh fix
Like thighs being workshopped you learn more
When you're not up when someone else is
Ghats how'll you'll learn Zoe old middle dads afar dfhfhrn

aaaahnn suffer a eld

Wlbbl Jo o ognownk wl cy the my kw. Way tue k f James
into. Wand parKeet opportunky ridding & keys Rm
crowd. Of DNA dot sleet clAiror jabd dloakrnf sea din
the swimming pok no knew our as lAtty for the cross v
droll loon fjellkrlPqt afnwt lend g w dieq nth e wAre fjnc
Dell drool rrjdnnabcimpanntiej f plant companigiwbs
xompacnis don't stake wzkfosn witei foe they'd n shrugs
dor beak Hhh fix

Onthughngto mympwnmisic one Lerner
Onthughngto mympwnmisic one Lerner
I Igbo bi as Leif eng of um um owns of
I Igbo bi as Leif eng of um um owns of
I FBI nth I as Leif wing to um own Mao mp
I FBI nth I as Leif wing to um own Mao mp
I thight. Is Leif

Emmy to um on fiturl
I thight. Is Leif Emmy to um on fiturl
Inhi
o we lent enigma to own soap
Inhi o we lent enigma to own soap
I thithn I we leitmen g to lyown music
I thithn I we leitmen g to lyown music
I thoughinwa leitmen gmtlpw ms ms
I thoughinwa leitmen gmtlpw ms ms
I thigh t I wan lent ding to Daniel spannp
I thigh t I wan lent ding to Daniel spannp
I thur knwankpranlsktnw corps vymwynpwnmisicp
I thur knwankpranlsktnw corps vymwynpwnmisicp
O thight inwanlsotenk g to my own sale
O thight inwanlsotenk g to my own sale

Thottnt I as Moscow it to known of
Thottnt I as Moscow it to known of
The best thought I was profs IV to gmwonmsick
The best thought I was profs IV to gmwonmsick
Pre is walled diet uolsn nooks
Pre is walled diet uolsn nooks
Dassnf daaarn guiros finthug FBIdmrhwtt lentie oeny
    Xmas nmh own way
Dassnf daaarn guiros finthug FBIdmrhwtt lentie oeny
    Xmas nmh own way
Muddy candy w. Newbe stow efn

new is job
Muddy candy w. Newbe stow efn new is job
Dental cost who pro irons
sfhfjn lnrpwlxamsnt z fond
Dental cost who pro irons sfhfjn lnrpwlxamsnt z fond
The pros is umm knspria h Fu k regent
The pros is umm knspria h Fu k regent
He lord is my ck
Log Maria cermochaAel
He lord is my ck
Log Maria cermochaAel
The Los is my cm
Licitly
The Los is my cm
Licitly
One a kmetionMf andten army g wtottwnx I z worked pup
Sophia Philadelphia Philadelphia Moore kevinrr hardly
mcveyg pica and y Tbarifn Kyleebennentn off ll
One a kmetionMf andten army g wtottwnx I z worked pup
Sophia Philadelphia Philadelphia Moore kevinrr hardly

mcveyg pica and y Tbarifn Kyleebennentn off ll
Snap surpmfonsceynxlosjneisnthenwhstn what aerogels
wit. You pepos you dot news to e Ann all em youndt never
call Lenin kyabr gol u h stuff just wain for menti go it Zhou
or popular sour ebb wifny. Begat edauy y baggage earth
baggwfdj ready keys

gotal a utnsnappnngn
Ntnt
Snap surpmfonsceynxlosjneisnthenwhstn what aerogels
    wit. You pepos
you dot news to e Ann all em youndt never call Lenin
kyabr gol u h stuff just wain for menti go it Zhou or
popular sour ebb wifny. Begat edauy y baggage earth
baggwfdj ready keys gotal a utnsnappnngn
Ntnt
Haven't wr all been hw before know IA kind of ally but I
    wngormaomntungmwninw
Haven't wr all been hw before know IA kind of ally but I
    wngormaomntungmwninw
Au ic cyp n gpjyo wtb each other int poke kn it ye Ole
    tpmalabo xch oh Ty
Au ic cyp n gpjyo wtb each other int poke kn it ye Ole
    tpmalabo xch oh Ty
By turoneunyqnymeontmek Mao any it renal townlnoth
By turoneunyqnymeontmek Mao any it renal townlnoth

STATE

sea-blanches grow enabling
the fungible shore likewise
chromatic awake the hedge-sparrow

feeds the cuckoo difference
who rose shedding spring
who upland rose *mildewed*

the white wheat the tran-
substantiated gusting
wheat who reaped

faded the coat of
furious of
in light of things

SEA OF LAND

The strand was lifted before spring was here
And carried in the water by the land
And her prefigurement pushed toward her
Against wind. There afternoon found
Light broadcast toward it over the bending
Of the sea, separate and clean.
She caught up in that garment led the sea
To a low brook and left it
For men to bide their bitter hours by
And hurt the waves with chiming voices.
Announced in light as wide as fallen
They turned to stand in dune grass facing
Their natural banks and sand wrecked their brows.
Covered by the sand was a wave of time
And they passed through it crying while moving.

OROMETRY

Among wind-hills the orphelin
Galloped through the air orphreyed.
"Livelong, sun. Livelong, orpine."
The hills flashed. And his tenor orpit,
He wished with God the wind orra
And also the planets in the orrery.

The ortet is the fosterer of the orrery,
Ramets of smiling youth now orphelin
Emblem of the homespun, tidal orbit—
"The sand in human stripes," he opined
Upon dismounting Orthangle, his steed orrath.
The waves made orphrey-web.

He raised his hand and felled the orphrey-web.
How far he'd ranged! When passenger with playmates for
    orrest,
The carriage orthoclase oped on the water orphelin.
One pinned him while the rest in strains orthian
Prayed for sun. But the moon was out of orbit
And the sky a spread orpine.

Knowing for whom he pined,
He sat and watched the shredded orphrey ebb.
Other forms of relief were mountainous or, under, of Orphic
Solemnities. To Orthangle he practiced on his orphion,

Against the waves which rose in high obit
At apex sparkling orsellate.

"Orright, waves, attend my orisons late,
Fore sunned to shifting orsedue."
Unheard, mid dunes, he pierced a patch of orchids
And was pierced. "I cannot see." Yet night was wide with
    ornament,
And he adopted as Orion
In winter, the constellation orthic.

Below the ocean, snow sank in waves of polyhedrons,
And, springlike, otters' daughters and sons
Swam from shore, sketching orbits
For show, splashing. The parents thanked Orion.
"Shooting stars, stroke their falling hair to orphrey!
Our children deadened by dew."

The orphelin dressed in orphrey
Against black (the dead orbit). Mechanically
Orra, he on Orthangle quested among pines.

NEUTRALIZATION

Now you scale a wave
Of empty sand, early
For winter,
Son of sea, sibling
Past, present and future.
From here, in your raised
Pit, bound by dune
Grasses, barred
Patterns of plovers declare
Death a majesty to bear.

LAND OF REASONING

In the clutches of song the survivors
Enter the earth no longer looking
For those they have lost that was
Another time even the underworld changes

We will find ourselves giving more
Attention to the underworld
Its landscape visible and action
What comes after existence after

Where is the meadow rampant
We were written of and wrote of
That is where action already the lord
Sang and did not appear

In the spring he will not appear that
Is what we have to understand when
We watch the time of day the lord
Sang the hardest task now facing us

What will later face us he sang early on
Early on in the life of the lord
A woodlark thrashes among the blea hedge
This is what life held for me
And encloses itself

ACT WITHOUT WORDS

      We cannot
store it. A writing up against water

One is almost not even there

      The flood
comes either way

         Gentleness a
    letting in
of that which is already
there, the gray

deployment of the wave

above the archway

And Lot sat in the gate peradventure

And they said *again*

And pulled Lot into the middle distance among them

I can't go anywhere until you become thither

And sent Lot out of the midst of the overthrow

Either way she's disappearing

Said through
rain would be slower.
God of the present
festival: *Will
not, will no*t

So that they wearied themselves to the door

What it means to make more than one thing, to make two
    things

where it blurs of its own volition

They put the deal away—very early after
it was made

There is an outpacing

The sand like a blind
shuttled over the body

falling away

Two questions about bird-
song. One, is there birdsong (over there) in anguish

each rung the light   lens flare

As the active is transgressed. Mercy
seeing. Her putting food in her mouth simply.
The pushed-back [covering] asked to do more
than it might

You cannot bury yourself

In the car—gathered russet of the city ahead
—ahead again—I think of that music—how it is
unreachable—really, if you try to reach it—how it
could save us. The city can be reached. It can
be like music ahead of us

How the fabric is unreachable.
Socrates says that grasping is the same
as shackling—and we, in our beauty, have given
the English name shackling, like birds
over chain-link—cry or no—
and the name-giver always finds fault
with that. Now what wants
to grasp the flow, Socrates
says, is called *blaberon*

The horizon can be forgotten and there.
God of hover.
He takes a shot and walks into it. Water
washing away from the rock completely

Freedom is what we want

The wind destroyed itself to be with you

No music. Still, there would be relevance

Towns are extremely important. The line is into the town

out of which here is merely disappearance

How did this happen?

Wind holding back all the bells

I left all of the books

Even if it doesn't, one can *not* look

Look. On the contrary

And let us not forget what echo means

The two hillsides converge on his head

We can do that
We can know nothing

They broke into each other
a minute ago

There are many screens

my disappearance—which is still
happening—my appearance

This story is very beautiful

Living would be possible

to come from the creation is to destroy

no no I mean I would destroy

The waves cannot but touch
where they have been.
This is breaking. We must always re-

ceding to keep the thing
whole. Something we can't touch.
We must keep walking out to sea

Soon there is nothing

The water came so close today
I thought of you

The earth will take me back again even as it
itself disappears

It can change

There are distances

[Do that to me]

The lines will burst where they fall

POSSIBLE EXPERIENCE

under the nettle the strawberry, winders
     within the site what was throstle song, the
future tied back with a ribbon,
the sea a single flag,
with her hand she is history she
sews stars under stars on her hand,
     the shore the table in flames,
she cuts her hair, that burns, she cuts
the ribbon in her hair

RARE EARTHS

Playing with his phone in her
Hand, frosty kit, a cloud in private
Public waves that Foxconn bundles, one after
Another with assumptions, no
Compromise, promise with me your content
Will return in netting over time, filming grainy
Footage, her focus broke
The waves on a velvet hunt, a wave from a
Beached girl, pissing a hole
For shit older than anger, a fox
In hell, whose broken
Heart would make me mine

HOPE MOUNTAIN

No less ice sheared my face. It was
my face that had discovered, then disowned,
sea. Could not stand, in its twitch, waves
could not be stilled or sheared to sand.
A scuttling nomenclature, its frothy
bits, in which I stood disarmed and posed
among some growing buds behind me.
White on my back, a white glowing.
A color entrained by minuscule
light—soon size of dream is enough.

Early it is enough, white sand,
no less the sky. The sand covers more. Its
availability, false graininess,
covers more—is washed more away.
You traveled from another place, another
beacon, the place you are, are reading
from. Which is the same, this
sand. Your head restrained by dew and its reminder.
A morning comes. A morning comes the plight,
shakes robins from the tree's attrition

and then carefully is gone. Pushed from the
shore. Your wet hands. Later the land again

received. No less than salt. And she turned back.
How many times has the story been read?
The human is capable of looking
at another's back and marching. It was warm
there. The crumbs bothered me. I said come in
and I fucked. An open pocket, a rain
on my hands. How I lasted. Joining the look
with grass. Enough for a hill or mound

less above than below the ground. Pulling
through sand I found it, plastic, like a painting
late style, as painting always was,
of sitting beside a pool, splashing its
face, sounding out its face. Alone among the
air, or its repose. A calm scene, middle-
focused, self-aware. Blinking at transports,
the trains or films waiting, following and
carrying. Sun made the trains, miniature,
sent the bodies, next to coal.

Aside the city I declined and wept.
The day flashed. The problem,
impotence, was flesh. The prior generation
too much of flesh, which wanted repetition
of love, not its outcry. Then on
the sand, crying, for impossibility,
and the man standing back above on
the hill. Wringing his breath. The grass then
looked down greener, subtler. Then flourishing
the springtide, volumetrics released back up.

HARPES ET LUZ

soon, fumiter-crowned, you bore the strown
hedge on water,
        where was the center under ashes,
and the sparrow before
appearance,

where is the hedge,
from the hedge,
        said the sparrow,
quick-
set, the hedge bruised

with leaves, floating, and the tortured
grew, and those before appearance,
        like waves,
decayed, bent over,

again, you said,
where is the hedge, said the sparrow,

where whit,
said *whit-*
age, whitecaps,
white cliffs, then you crossed the logical sand

ACKNOWLEDGMENTS

Thank you to *Adult, American Letters & Commentary, The Arcadia Project: North American Postmodern Pastoral, ARMED CELL, Bestoned, Boston Review, Chicago Review, Colorado Review, Conjunctions, Denver Quarterly, DIAGRAM, The Harvard Advocate, Hi Zero, Lana Turner: A Journal of Poetry and Opinion, nthposition, Parcel, Web Conjunctions,* and *Zoland Poetry,* where these poems previously appeared.

Thank you to Chris Balmer, Janette Cantor, Jorie Graham, Jess Laser, Alex Linsker, Jessica Marsh, Deborah Moses, Jeff Nagy, Geoffrey G. O'Brien, Giulio Pertile, Dan Poppick, Margaret Ross, and Peter Sacks.

1987
Elton Glaser, *Tropical Depressions*
Michael Pettit, *Cardinal Points*

1988
Bill Knott, *Outremer*
Mary Ruefle, *The Adamant*

1989
Conrad Hilberry, *Sorting the Smoke*
Terese Svoboda, *Laughing Africa*

1990
Philip Dacey, *Night Shift at the Crucifix Factory*
Lynda Hull, *Star Ledger*

1991
Greg Pape, *Sunflower Facing the Sun*
Walter Pavlich, *Running near the End of the World*

1992
Lola Haskins, *Hunger*
Katherine Soniat, *A Shared Life*

1993

Tom Andrews, *The Hemophiliac's Motorcycle*

Michael Heffernan, *Love's Answer*

John Wood, *In Primary Light*

1994

James McKean, *Tree of Heaven*

Bin Ramke, *Massacre of the Innocents*

Ed Roberson, *Voices Cast Out to Talk Us In*

1995

Ralph Burns, *Swamp Candles*

Maureen Seaton, *Furious Cooking*

1996

Pamela Alexander, *Inland*

Gary Gildner, *The Bunker in the Parsley Fields*

John Wood, *The Gates of the Elect Kingdom*

1997

Brendan Galvin, *Hotel Malabar*

Leslie Ullman, *Slow Work through Sand*

1998

Kathleen Peirce, *The Oval Hour*

Bin Ramke, *Wake*

Cole Swensen, *Try*

1999

Larissa Szporluk, *Isolato*

Liz Waldner, *A Point Is That Which Has No Part*

2000
Mary Leader, *The Penultimate Suitor*

2001
Joanna Goodman, *Trace of One*
Karen Volkman, *Spar*

2002
Lesle Lewis, *Small Boat*
Peter Jay Shippy, *Thieves' Latin*

2003
Michele Glazer, *Aggregate of Disturbances*
Dainis Hazners, *(some of) The Adventures of Carlyle, My Imaginary Friend*

2004
Megan Johnson, *The Waiting*
Susan Wheeler, *Ledger*

2005
Emily Rosko, *Raw Goods Inventory*
Joshua Marie Wilkinson, *Lug Your Careless Body out of the Careful Dusk*

2006
Elizabeth Hughey, *Sunday Houses the Sunday House*
Sarah Vap, *American Spikenard*

2008
Andrew Michael Roberts, *something has to happen next*
Zach Savich, *Full Catastrophe Living*

2009

Samuel Amadon, *Like a Sea*

Molly Brodak, *A Little Middle of the Night*

2010

Julie Hanson, *Unbeknownst*

L. S. Klatt, *Cloud of Ink*

2011

Joseph Campana, *Natural Selections*

Kerri Webster, *Grand & Arsenal*

2012

Stephanie Pippin, *The Messenger*

2013

Eric Linsker, *La Far*

Alexandria Peary, *Control Bird Alt Delete*